WEEKLY WR READER®

EARLY LEARNING LIBRARY

How Plants Grow/Cómo crecen las plantas

How Apple Trees Grow/
Cómo crecen los manzanos

by/por Joanne Mattern

Reading consultant/Consultora de lectura:
Susan Nations, M.Ed.,
author, literacy coach,
and consultant in literacy development/
autora, tutora de alfabetización,
y consultora de desarrollo de la lectura

Please visit our web site at: www.earlyliteracy.cc
For a free color catalog describing Weekly Reader® Early Learning Library's list
of high-quality books, call 1-877-445-5824 (USA) or 1-800-387-3178 (Canada).
Weekly Reader® Early Learning Library's fax: (414) 336-0164.

Library of Congress Cataloging-in-Publication Data

Mattern, Joanne, 1963-
  [How apple trees grow. (Spanish & English)]
  How apple trees grow = Cómo crecen los manzanos / Joanne Mattern.
    p. cm. — (How plants grow = Cómo crecen las plantas)
  Includes bibliographical references and index.
  ISBN 0-8368-6460-3 (lib.bdg.)
  ISBN 0-8368-6467-0 (softcover)
  1. Apples—Growth—Juvenile literature. 2. Apples—Development—Juvenile literature.
I. Title: Cómo crecen los manzanos. II. Title.
QK495.M78M3618   2006
583'.73—dc22   2005032233

This edition first published in 2006 by
Weekly Reader® Early Learning Library
A Member of the WRC Media Family of Companies
330 West Olive Street, Suite 100
Milwaukee, WI 53212 USA

Copyright © 2006 by Weekly Reader® Early Learning Library

Managing editor: Valerie J. Weber
Art direction: Tammy West
Cover design and page layout: Kami Strunsee
Translators: Tatiana Acosta and Guillermo Gutiérrez
Picture research: Cisley Celmer

Picture credits: Cover, p. 5 © Gibson Stock Photography; p. 7 © Michael Newman/PhotoEdit;
p. 9 © Nigel Cattlin/Holt Studios/Photo Researchers, Inc.; p. 11 © Maryann Frazier/Photo
Researchers, Inc.; p. 13 © Patrick Reddy/America 24-7/Getty Images; p. 15 © Ann Cutting/
Botanica/Getty Images; p. 17 © Alan and Linda Detrick/Photo Researchers, Inc.; p. 19
© Ann Ackerman/Taxi/Getty Images; p. 21 © Richard Hutchings/PhotoEdit

Printed in the United States of America

1 2 3 4 5 6 7 8 9 10 09 08 07 06

42793

Note to Educators and Parents

Reading is such an exciting adventure for young children! They are beginning to integrate their oral language skills with written language. To encourage children along the path to early literacy, books must be colorful, engaging, and interesting; they should invite the young reader to explore both the print and the pictures.

How Plants Grow is a new series designed to introduce young readers to the life cycle of familiar plants. In simple, easy-to-read language, each book explains how a specific plant begins, grows, and changes.

Each book is specially designed to support the young reader in the reading process. The familiar topics are appealing to young children and invite them to read — and reread — again and again. The full-color photographs and enhanced text further support the student during the reading process.

In addition to serving as wonderful picture books in schools, libraries, homes, and other places where children learn to love reading, these books are specifically intended to be read within an instructional guided reading group. This small group setting allows beginning readers to work with a fluent adult model as they make meaning from the text. After children develop fluency with the text and content, the book can be read independently. Children and adults alike will find these books supportive, engaging, and fun!

— Susan Nations, M.Ed., author, literacy coach,
and consultant in literacy development

Nota para los maestros y los padres

¡Leer es una aventura tan emocionante para los niños pequeños! A esta edad están comenzando a integrar su manejo del lenguaje oral con el lenguaje escrito. Para animar a los niños en el camino de la lectura incipiente, los libros deben ser coloridos, estimulantes e interesantes; deben invitar a los jóvenes lectores a explorar la letra impresa y las ilustraciones.

Cómo crecen las plantas es una nueva colección diseñada para presentar a los jóvenes lectores el ciclo de vida de plantas muy conocidas. Cada libro explica, en un lenguaje sencillo y fácil de leer, cómo nace, se desarrolla y cambia una planta específica.

Cada libro está especialmente diseñado para ayudar a los jóvenes lectores en el proceso de lectura. Los temas familiares llaman la atención de los niños y los invitan a leer — y releer — una y otra vez. Las fotografías a todo color y el tamaño de la letra ayudan aún más al estudiante en el proceso de lectura.

Además de servir como maravillosos libros ilustrados en escuelas, bibliotecas, hogares y otros lugares donde los niños aprenden a amar la lectura, estos libros han sido especialmente concebidos para ser leídos en un grupo de lectura guiada. Este contexto permite que los lectores incipientes trabajen con un adulto que domina la lectura mientras van determinando el significado del texto. Una vez que los niños dominan el texto y el contenido, el libro puede ser leído de manera independiente. ¡Estos libros les resultarán útiles, estimulantes y divertidos a niños y a adultos por igual!

— Susan Nations, M.Ed., autora, tutora de alfabetización, y
consultora de desarrollo de la lectura

Where do apple trees come from? They come from seeds.

¿De dónde vienen los manzanos? Vienen de las semillas.

5

Plant some apple seeds. In a few years, a tree will grow.

Planta unas semillas de manzano. En unos pocos años, saldrá un árbol.

What is that? It is a **bud**.

¿Qué es eso? Es un **capullo**.

9

The bud opens into a
pretty flower. Look at
the pretty **blossom**!

El capullo se abre y se
convierte en una bella flor.
¡Mira qué linda!

11

The blossom falls off. Now there is an apple on the tree.

La flor se cae. Ahora hay una manzana en el árbol.

13

The apple grows bigger
and bigger.

La manzana se hace más
y más grande.

The apple changes color. It was green. Then it turns red.

La manzana cambia de color. Era verde. Ahora se vuelve roja.

The apples are **ripe**. They are
ready to pick.

Las manzanas están **maduras**.
Ya se pueden recoger.

Apples taste so good!

¡Las manzanas saben
muy bien!

21

Glossary

blossom — a flower
bud — part of a plant that grows into a flower or a leaf
ripe — ready to pick and eat
seeds — parts of a plant that grow into new plants

Glosario

capullo — parte de una planta que se convierte en una flor o una hoja
flor — parte de una planta que se forma al abrirse un capullo
madura — que se puede recoger y comer
semillas — partes de una planta que se convierten en nuevas plantas

For More Information/Más información

Books

Apples. Gail Gibbons (Holiday House)

I Am an Apple. Jean Marzollo (Scholastic)

Libros

Ana cultiva manzanas/Apple Farmer Annie: A Bilingual Edition in Spanish and English. Monica Wellington (Dutton Juvenile)

El manzanar/Apple Orchard. Heinemann Lee Y Aprende/Heinemann Read and Learn (series). Catherine Anderson (Heinemann)

Web Sites/Páginas web

U.S. Apple Association Kids Page/
Página infantil de la Asociación U.S. Apple
www.usapple.org/consumers/kids/index.shtml
This site includes information about apples and a coloring book too!
Esta página contiene información sobre las manzanas, ¡y un libro para colorear!

Index

Índice

About the Author

Joanne Mattern has written more than 150 books for children. Her favorite things to write about are animals, nature, history, sports, and famous people. Joanne also works in her local library. She lives in New York State with her husband, three daughters, and assorted pets. She enjoys animals, music, going to baseball games, reading, and visiting schools to talk about her books.

Información sobre la autora

Joanne Mattern ha escrito más de 150 libros para niños. Sus temas favoritos son los animales, la naturaleza, la historia, los deportes y la vida de personajes famosos. Además, Joanne trabaja en la biblioteca de su comunidad. Vive en el estado de Nueva York con su esposo, sus tres hijas y varias mascotas. A Joanne le gustan los animales, la música, ir al béisbol, leer y hacer visitas a las escuelas para hablar de sus libros.